Pretty Little Animals Coloring Book

€ 2023 by Selena L.L. Arnold All rights reserved.

Unauthorized use or reproduction of any portion of this book is strictly prohibited without the author's prior written consent, except for brief quotations allowed for book reviews.

ISBN: 9798866096138
Imprint: Independently published

This Book Belongs To:

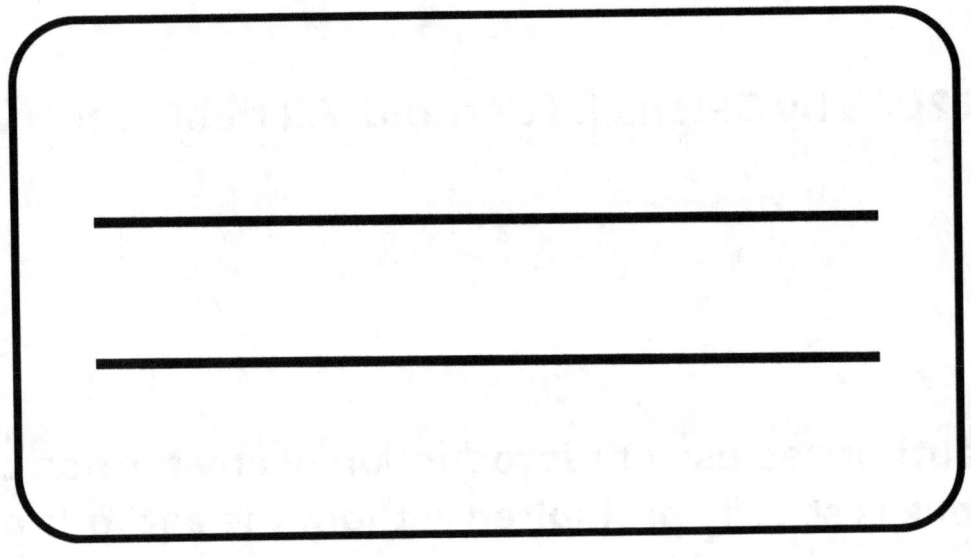

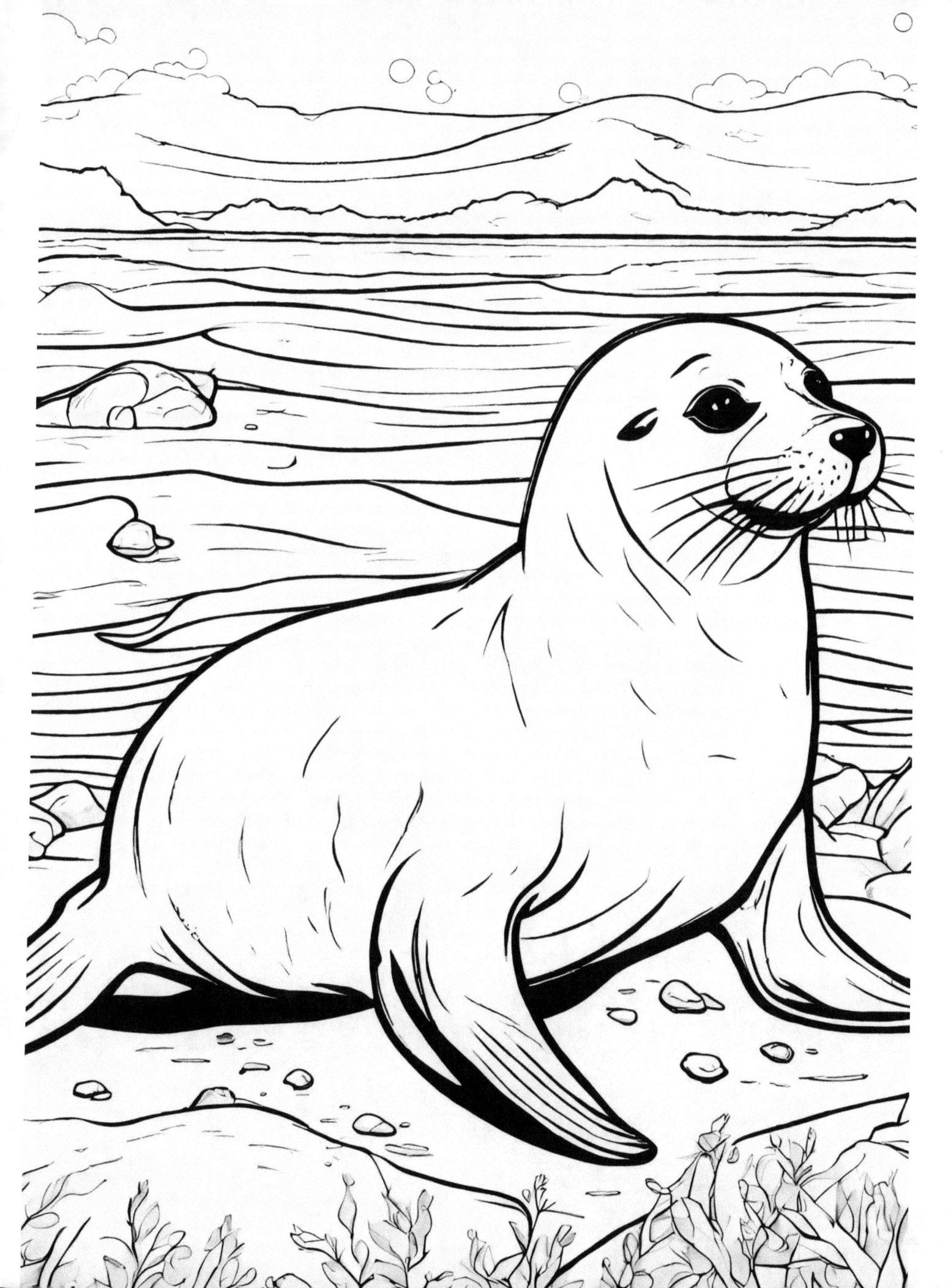

www.ingramcontent.com/pod-product-compliance
Lightning Source LLC
LaVergne TN
LVHW081616060526
838201LV00054B/2275